GROSSEST
ANIMAL TRICKS

Gareth Stevens
PUBLISHING

BY AGATHA GREGSON

Please visit our website, www.garethstevens.com. For a free color catalog of all our high-quality books, call toll free 1-800-542-2595 or fax 1-877-542-2596.

Library of Congress Cataloging-in-Publication Data

Gregson, Agatha, author.
 Grossest animal tricks / Agatha Gregson.
     pages cm. — (Ultimate animal defenses)
 Includes bibliographical references and index.
ISBN 978-1-4824-4445-2 (pbk.)
ISBN 978-1-4824-4386-8 (6 pack)
ISBN 978-1-4824-4427-8 (library binding)
1. Animal defenses—Juvenile literature. 2. Animal behavior—Juvenile literature. 3. Adaptation (Biology)—Juvenile literature. I. Title.
 QL759.G74 2017
 591.47—dc23
                                        2015021484

First Edition

Published in 2017 by
Gareth Stevens Publishing
111 East 14th Street, Suite 349
New York, NY 10003

Copyright © 2017 Gareth Stevens Publishing

Designer: Katelyn E. Reynolds
Editor: Therese Shea

Photo credits: Cover, p. 1 Wolfgang Poelzer/WaterFrame/Getty Images; cover, pp. 1–24 (background texture) vector illustration/Shutterstock.com; p. 5 (snake) worldswildlifewonders/Shutterstock.com; p. 5 (owl) Mark Bridger/Shutterstock.com; p. 5 (polar bear) Furtseff/Shutterstock.com; p. 7 Critterbiz/Shutterstock.com; p. 9 TOM MCHUGH/Science Source/Getty Images; p. 11 Tobias Bernhard/Oxford Scientific/Getty Images; p. 13 Cultura RM/George Karbus Photography/Getty Images; p. 15 John Cancalosi/Photolibrary/Getty Images; p. 17 Andrew Skolnick/Shutterstock.com; p. 19 Piotr Naskrecki/Minden Pictures/Getty Images; p. 20 reptiles4all/Shutterstock.com; p. 21 (whale) Reinhard Dirscherl/WaterFrame/Getty Images; p. 21 (vulture) Dave Montreuil/Shutterstock.com; p. 21 (newt) Sergio Gutierrez Getino/Shutterstock.com; p. 21 (potato bug) Ansis Klucis/Shutterstock.com.

Printed in the United States of America

CPSIA compliance information: Batch #CS16GS : For further information contact Gareth Stevens, New York, New York at 1-800-542-2595.

CONTENTS

Words in the glossary appear in **bold** type the first time they are used in the text.

EWWW . . . GROSS!

Has your brother or sister ever done anything so gross that you just wanted to leave them alone? Believe it or not, something similar happens in the wild! However, instead of your family acting gross "just because," an animal often does something we think is gross to **defend** itself from a predator. The nasty action is an **adaptation** that they **evolved** to survive in the wild. It's better to be gross than dead!

Are you ready for some really gross animal adaptations? Read on!

STINKY SKUNKS

Don't ever scare a skunk. Its best defense is a powerful one! A skunk's spray carries a terrible odor, or smell, that's very hard to wash off skin and fur.

The skunk produces the yellowish spray in **glands** in its body. When a skunk is frightened, it turns its back on the **threat**, raises its tail, and sprays up to 15 feet (4.6 m) away. The spray can be painful on an animal's face and may even blind them for a time. This gives the skunk enough time to get away.

SO WILD!

When a skunk's spray mixes with water, the odor gets even worse!

IT CAN TAKE A SKUNK A WEEK TO PRODUCE MORE SPRAY IN ITS BODY.

THERE ARE 11 SPECIES, OR KINDS, OF SKUNKS.

FOUL HAGFISH

Another name for the hagfish is the slime eel. However, slime eels aren't eels. They're fish without bones. This name is fitting in one way, though. The creatures secrete, or ooze, slime onto the outside of their body. Yuck!

A hagfish's body is lined with glands that produce matter that turns into slime when it touches water. When a predator tries to bite the hagfish, the fish gets away while the predator is left with a mouthful of slime! The slime may even **clog** the gills of predators, such as sharks.

SO WILD!

Hagfish slime is strong. Scientists think it could be used to make clothing someday!

SICKENING SEA CUCUMBERS

Sea cucumbers have soft bodies with no bones. There are more than 1,200 species in the world's oceans. Some live in shallow waters, while others like the deep.

Some sea cucumbers have a very unusual way to protect, or guard, themselves from enemies such as crabs, sea stars, and fish. They eject, or push out, sticky threads from their body to trap or **confuse** their predators. Others actually eject their body's **organs**! The gross matter may even be coated with toxins that can kill predators.

SO WILD!

Sea cucumbers also use camouflage as a way to hide from predators.

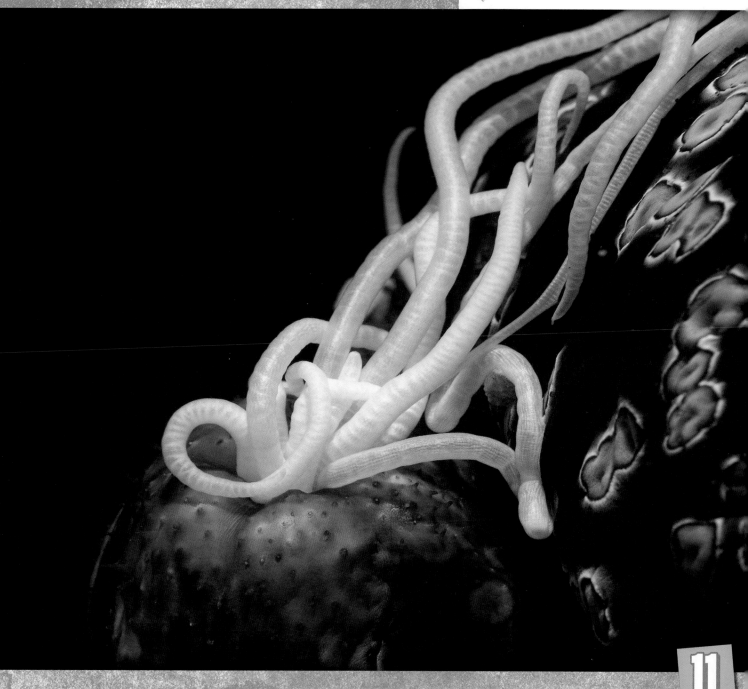

AWFUL FULMARS

The fulmar is a gray and white seabird that builds its nest on cliffs near the ocean. It eats all kinds of sea creatures, living or dead, and even eats trash. Because fulmar nests aren't hidden, parents and chicks need to be able to defend themselves. They do this by vomiting, or throwing up, on their predators!

When threatened by enemies such as eagles and falcons, fulmars can vomit fish oil from up to 5 feet (1.5 m) away. Not only does the vomit smell bad, it makes birds' feathers stick together.

SO WILD!

The fulmar's vomit can even cause feathers to lose their ability to help birds float and keep warm.

HORRIFYING HORNED LIZARDS

The horned lizard has a famous defense to scare away predators, but that doesn't make it any less shocking. It can shoot blood from its eyes!

The horned lizard lives in desert areas of western North America and Central America. Their many predators include hawks, snakes, lizards, dogs, wolves, and coyotes. When horned lizards are scared, they can fire blood at an enemy up to 3 feet (0.9 m) away. The blood may have a **chemical** in it that tastes bad to some predators, too.

ODIOUS OPOSSUMS

Opossums are small **marsupials** of North and South America that are usually active at night. Because of their size, they're prey to larger animals such as foxes, hawks, coyotes, and snakes. Luckily, opossums have several gross defenses to fight back.

When facing a predator, the small creature may burp, pee, and poop! If the predator still won't leave it alone, the opossum plays dead. It rolls over, becomes stiff, and gives off a terrible odor. Many predators decide an opossum isn't such a tasty meal after that!

THIS OPOSSUM, SCARED BY A DOG, PLAYS DEAD. IT'S NOT ACTUALLY PRETENDING, THOUGH. IT'S THE WAY ITS BODY DEALS WITH THREATS. IT MAY NOT "WAKE UP" FOR SEVERAL HOURS.

SO WILD!

Opossums seem to be **immune** to some kinds of snake **venom**. That's another useful adaptation.

GROSS GRASSHOPPERS

Grasshoppers are a tasty treat for many kinds of predators. However, some grasshopper species have a trick to really gross out their enemies. They eject foam onto their body! Not only does it look disgusting, it's also poisonous. This poison comes from plants that the grasshoppers eat, such as milkweed. A grasshopper stores the poison in its body until it feels threatened.

The koppie foam grasshopper of Africa is one species of distasteful grasshoppers with this adaptation. Birds and dogs have died after eating this foaming bug!

SO WILD!

The red coloring on a koppie foam grasshopper's body warns its enemies that it's poisonous.

DISGUSTING KOMODO DRAGONS

The lizards known as Komodo dragons have a really gross mouth. Their spit is filled with different **bacteria** that can kill their victims! Adult Komodo dragons don't have to worry about predators, but their babies do. They don't have deadly bites yet and are preyed upon by larger Komodo dragons.

So, a young Komodo dragon may roll around in the poop that remains of an older Komodo dragon's prey! This makes the smaller lizards smell so terrible that the big lizards leave them alone. Is this the grossest defense? You decide!

The large lizards called Komodo dragons are found only on islands in Indonesia in Southeast Asia.

GROSS-OUT!

The dwarf sperm whale ejects clouds of poop to hide its escape route from enemies.

The vulture throws up a terrible-smelling and burning vomit on enemies.

MORE GREAT ANIMAL DEFENSES

The Iberian ribbed newt pokes its ribs through its skin to make poisonous spikes.

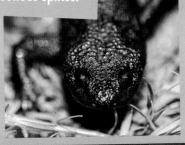

Potato beetle larvae roll in their own poisonous poop to protect themselves from predators.

21

GLOSSARY

adaptation: a change in a type of animal that makes it better able to live in its surroundings

bacteria: tiny creatures that can only be seen with a microscope

camouflage: colors or shapes in animals that allow them to blend in with their surroundings

chemical: matter that can be mixed with other matter to cause changes

clog: to block an opening

confuse: to mix up

defend: to guard against harm

evolve: to grow and change over time

gland: a body part that produces matter needed for a bodily function

immune: protected from something harmful

marsupial: a mammal whose young develop in a pouch on the mother's belly

organ: a body part that performs a certain function

threat: something likely to cause harm

venom: something an animal makes in its body that can harm other animals

FOR MORE INFORMATION

BOOKS

Clarke, Ginjer L. *Gross Out! Animals That Do Disgusting Things.* New York, NY: Grosset & Dunlap, 2006.

Gould, Francesca, and David Haviland. *Why Dogs Eat Poop: Gross But True Things You Never Knew About Animals.* New York, NY: G.P. Putnam's Sons, 2013.

Miller, Connie Colwell. *Disgusting Animals.* Mankato, MN: Capstone Press, 2007.

WEBSITES

Fooled by Nature: Fulmar Chick's Vomit
animals.howstuffworks.com/28383-fooled-by-nature-fulmar-chicks-vomit-video.htm
See a fulmar chick protect itself when it feels threatened.

World's Weirdest
video.nationalgeographic.com/video/weirdest-sea-cucumber
Watch a sea cucumber defend itself with its own guts!

INDEX